"You never know how strong you are until being strong is your only choice."
— Bob Marley

Hi!, I'm fluffy and I love to play. Have you ever gotten hurt while playing?

Last week I fell and got hurt

When I saw my leg, blood

was over there

Blood is made up of 3 main kinds of cells
Let's meet them!!

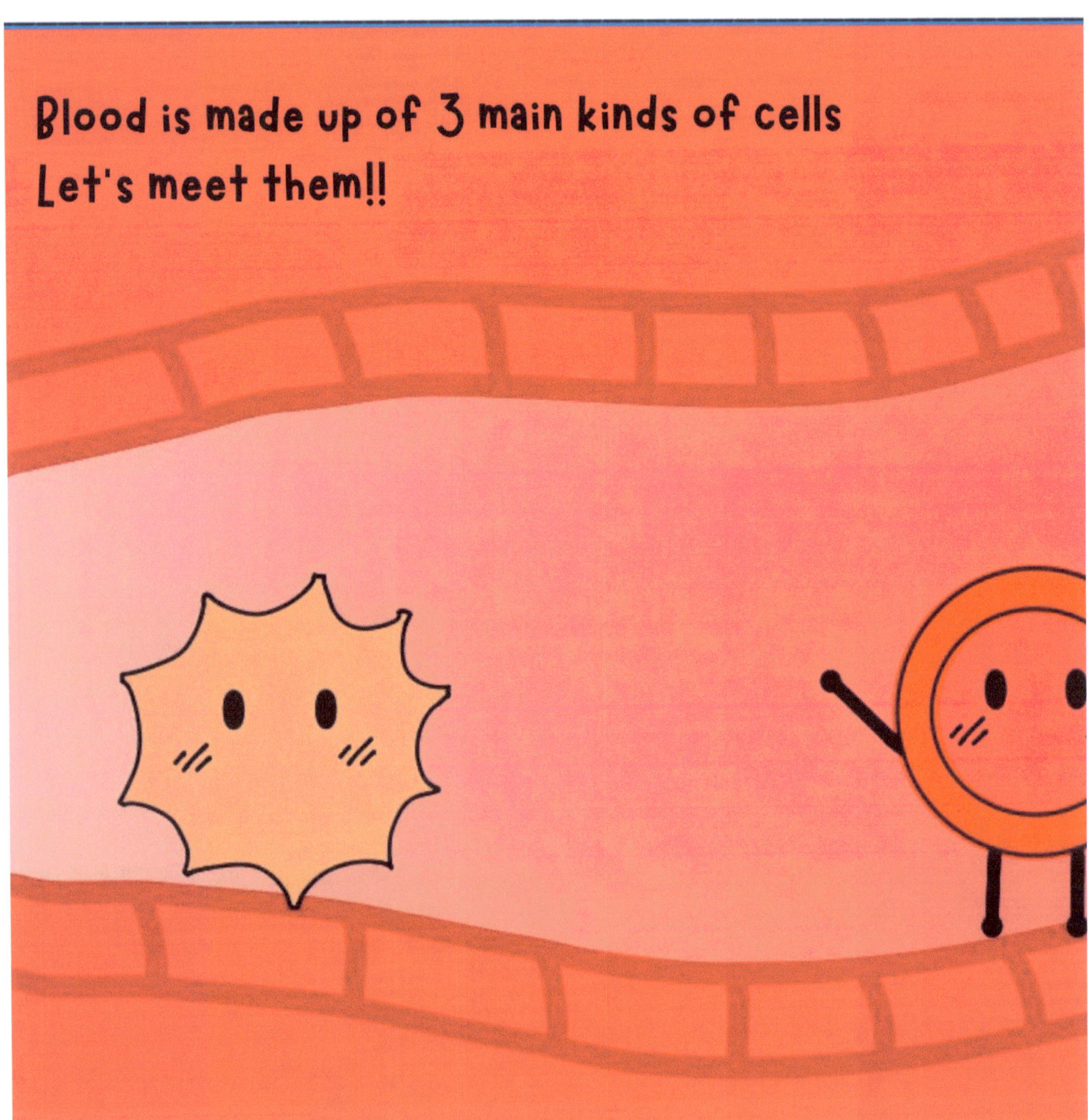

O₂

Hi!, I'm red blood cell

my job is to carry oxygen to your organs

O₂
O₂
O₂
O₂
LET'S GOO!

I'm white blood cell,
and I fight the germs in your body

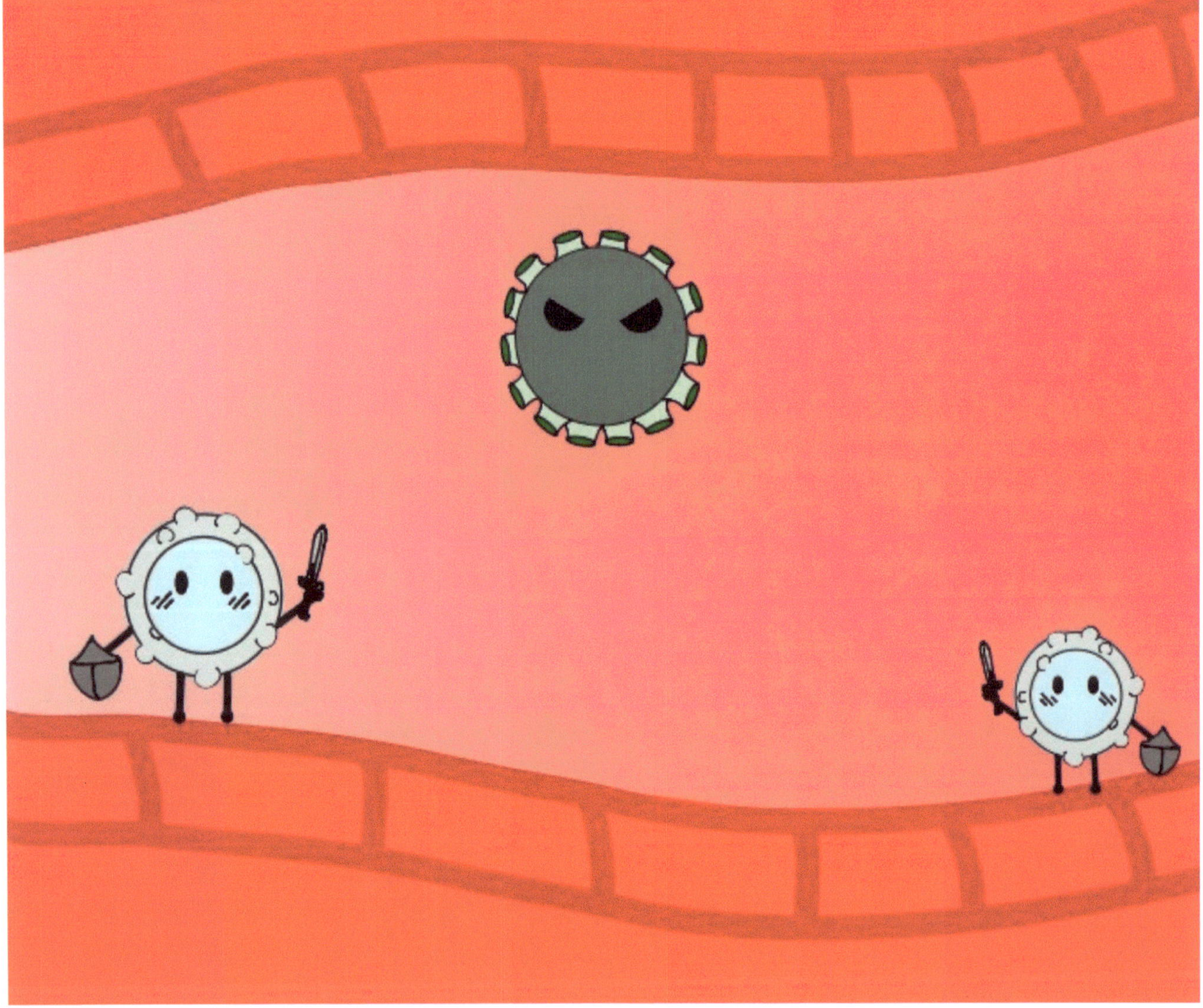

I WILL MAKE SURE ITS YOUR LAST DAY IN THE BODY

Heloooo,I'm a platelet
and I patch up the wounds when you get
hurt

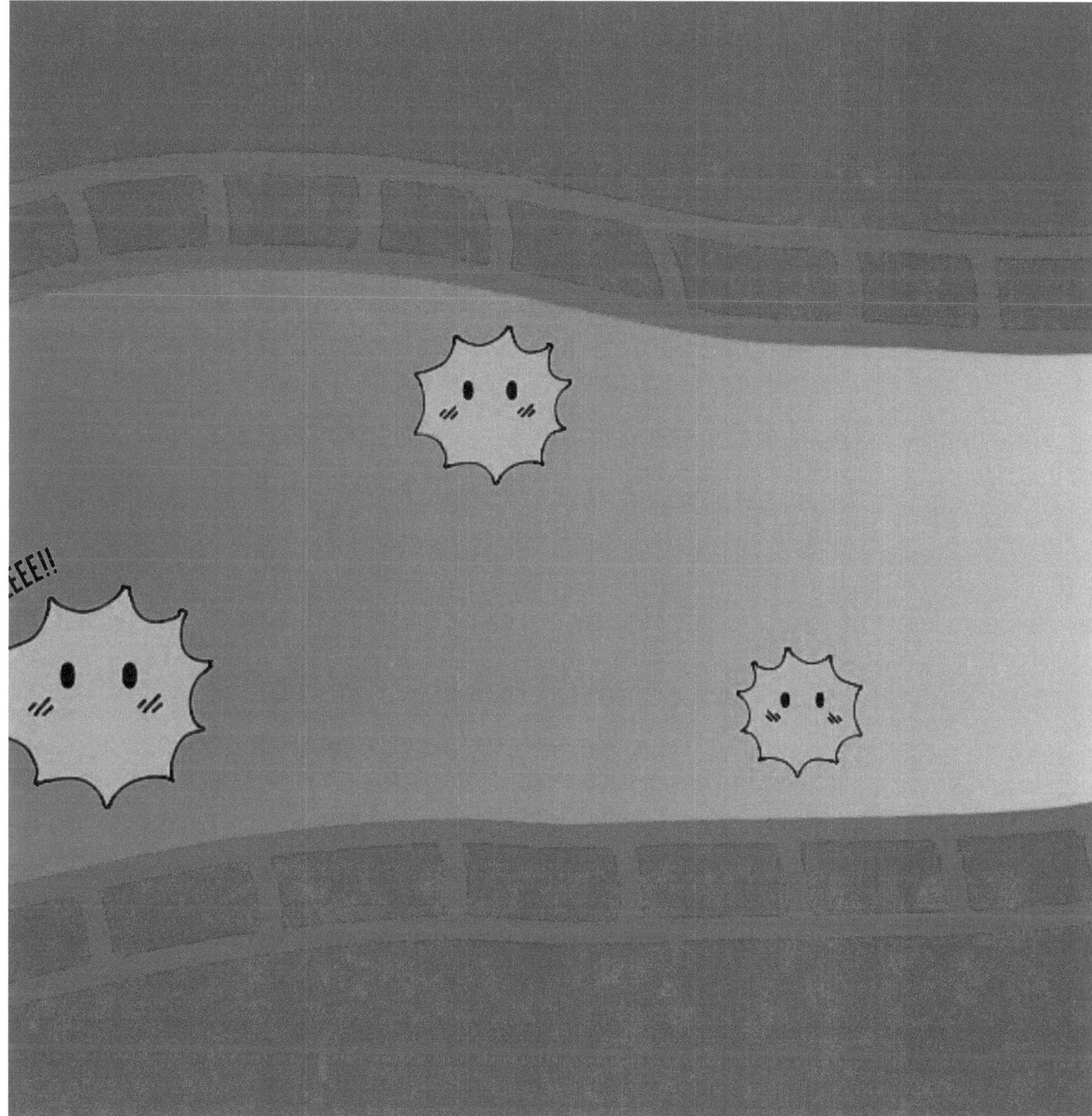
EEE!!

Our body is made up 206 bones which gives us structure

Bones have bone marrow which make the 3 different types of blood cells

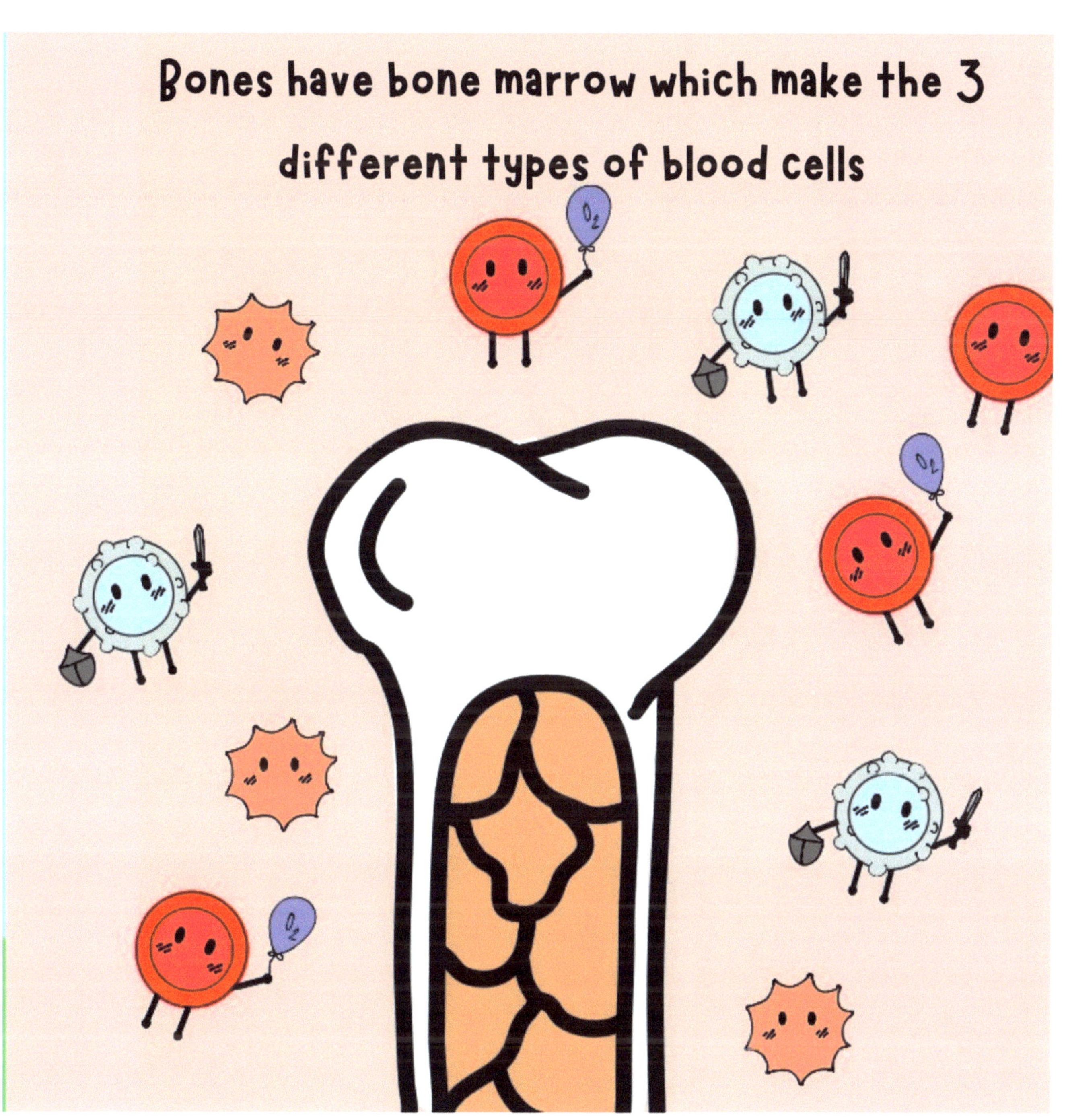

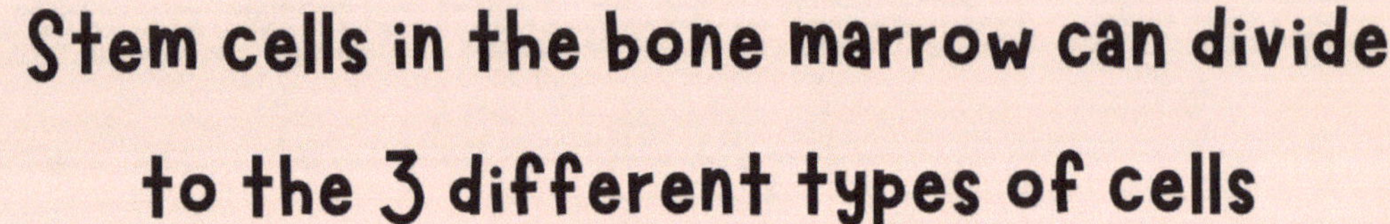

Stem cells in the bone marrow can divide to the 3 different types of cells

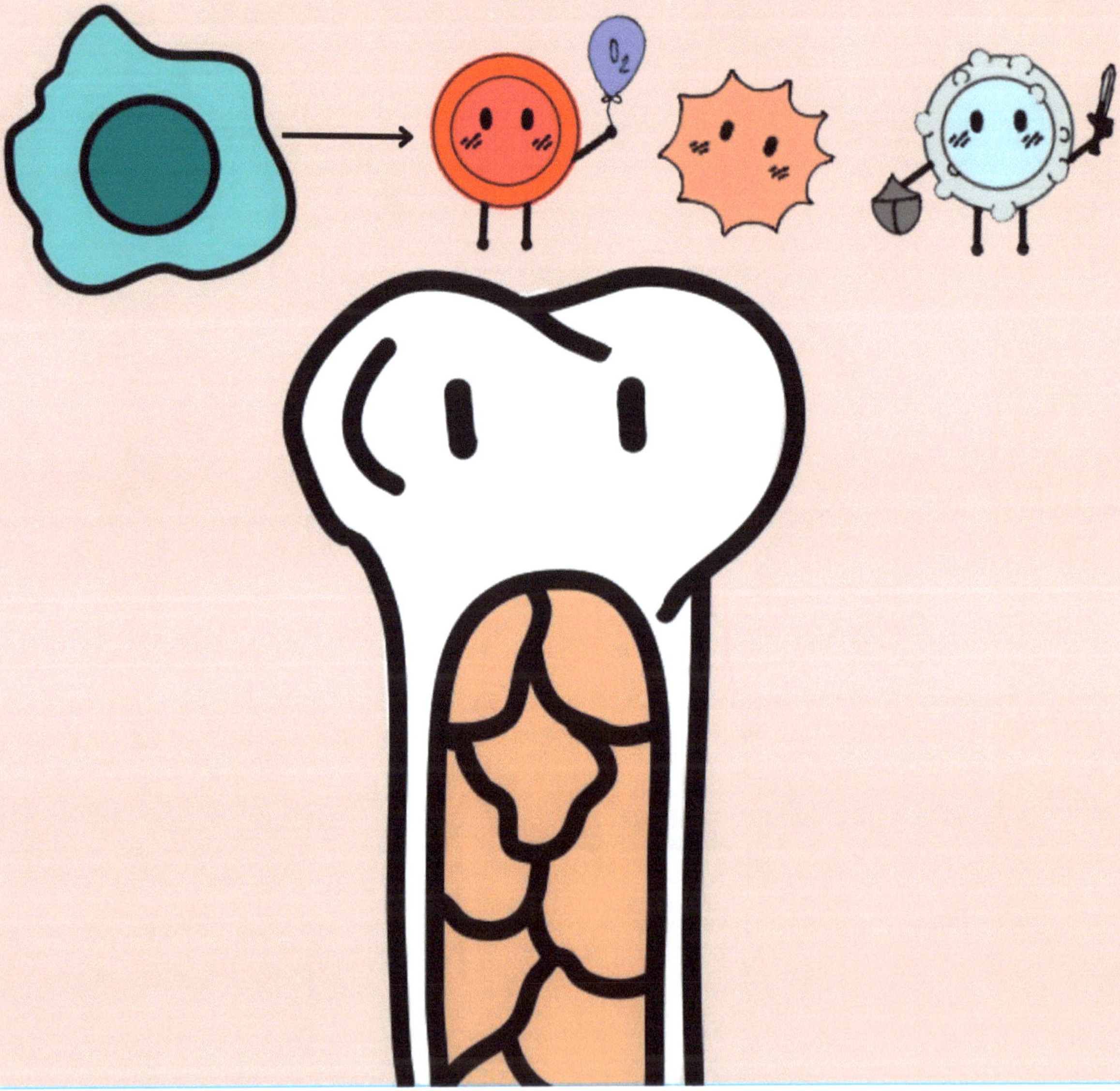

Example of a stem cell turning into a white blood cell

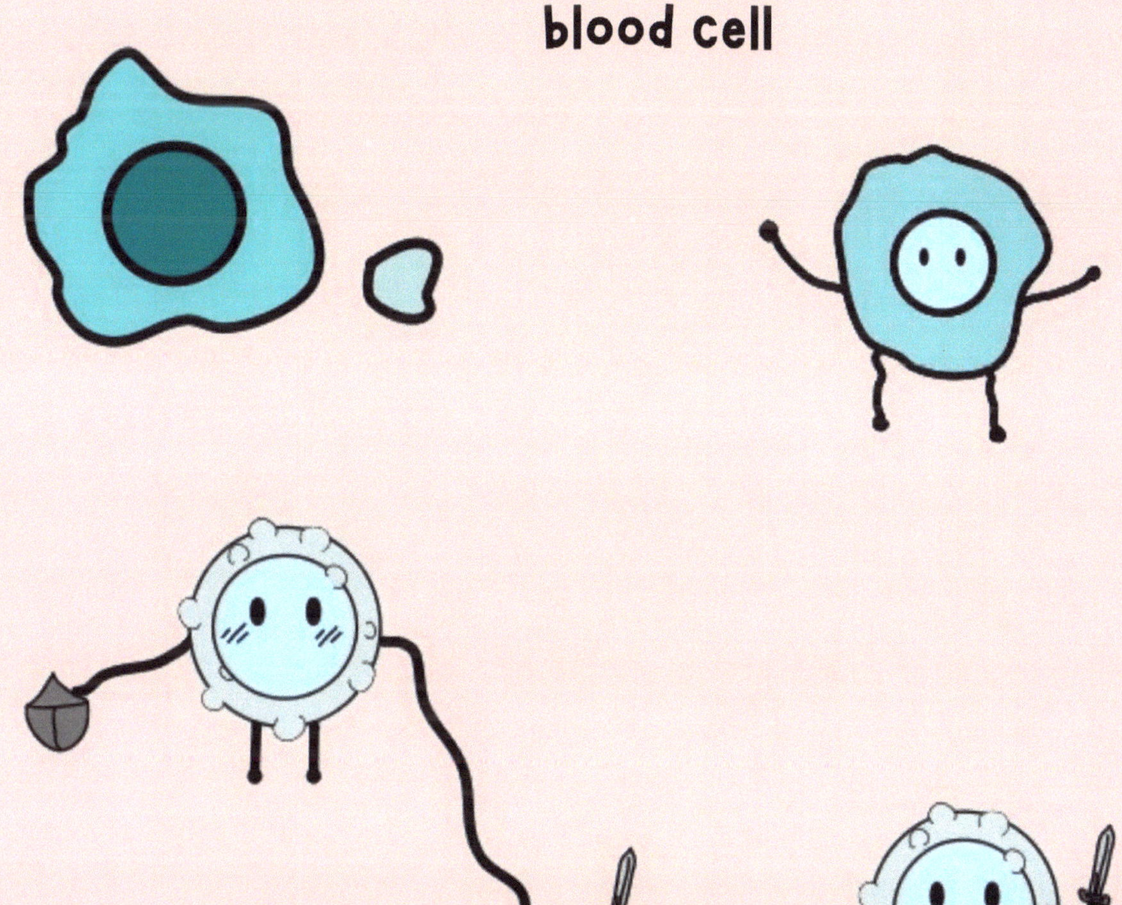

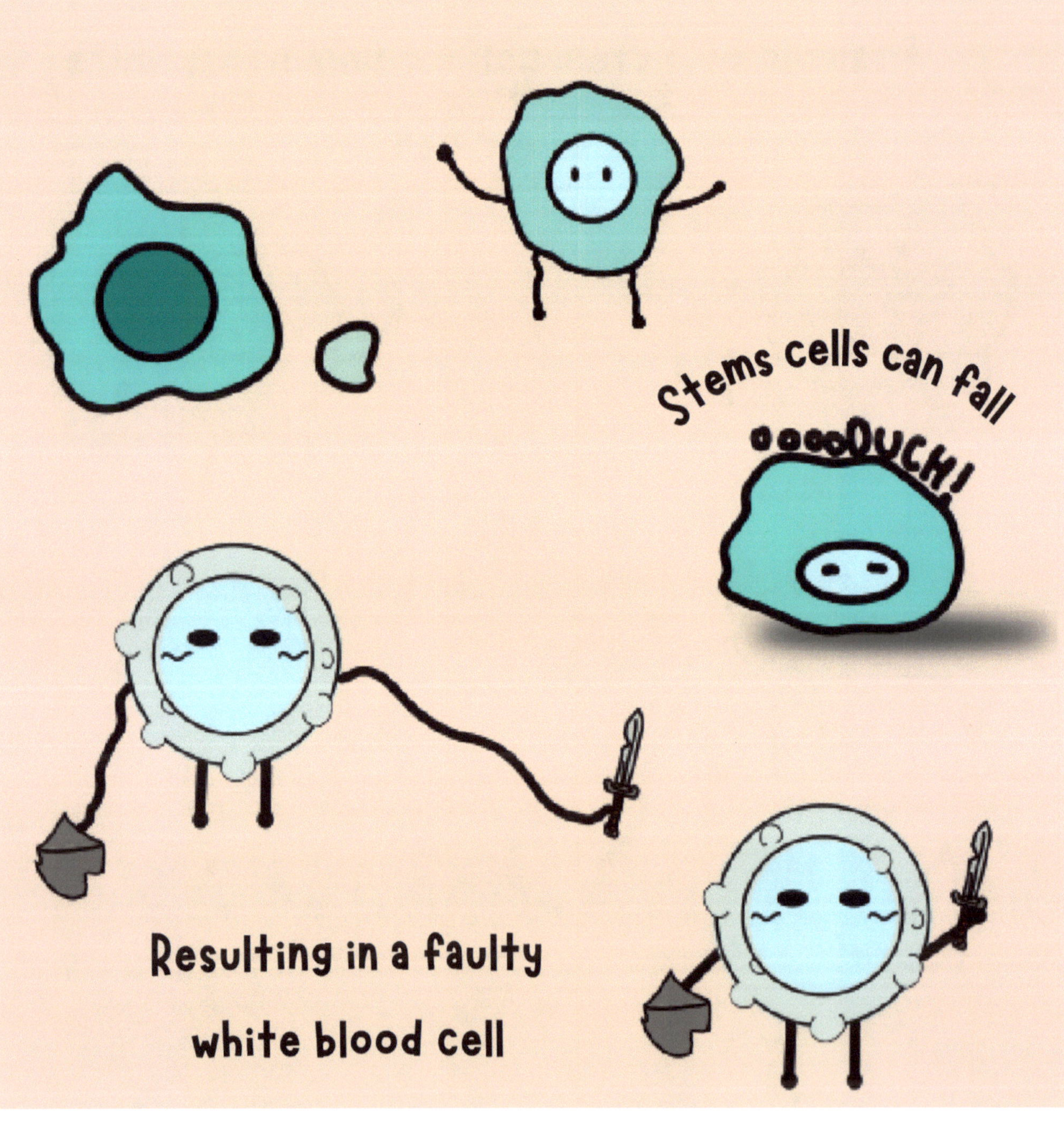
Stems cells can fall
oooDUCH!
Resulting in a faulty
white blood cell

These stem cells falling produce faulty cells

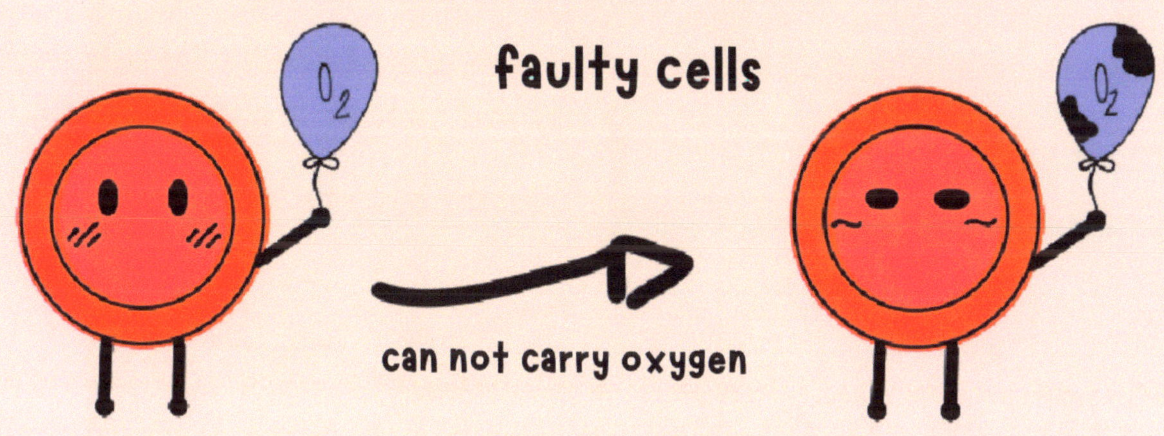

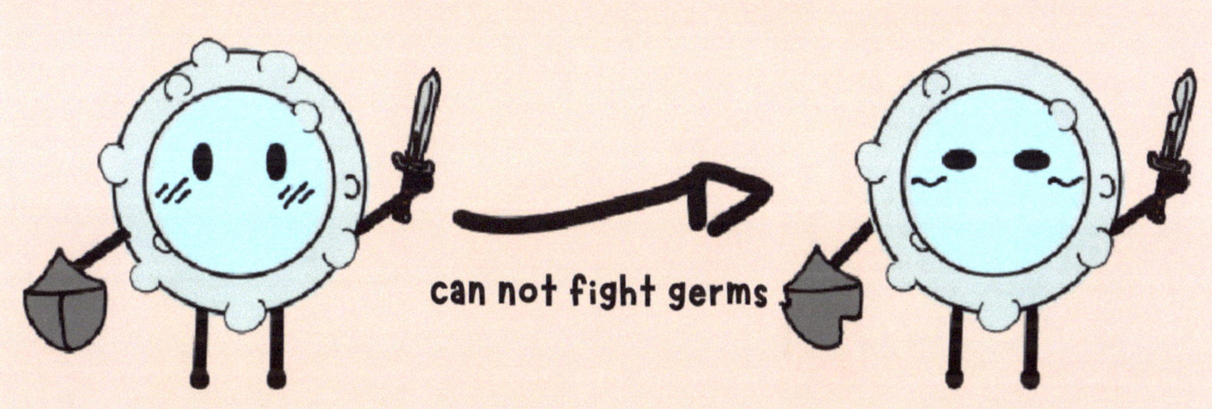

Blood cancer is a disease
caused by 3 main factors

FAULTY CELLS

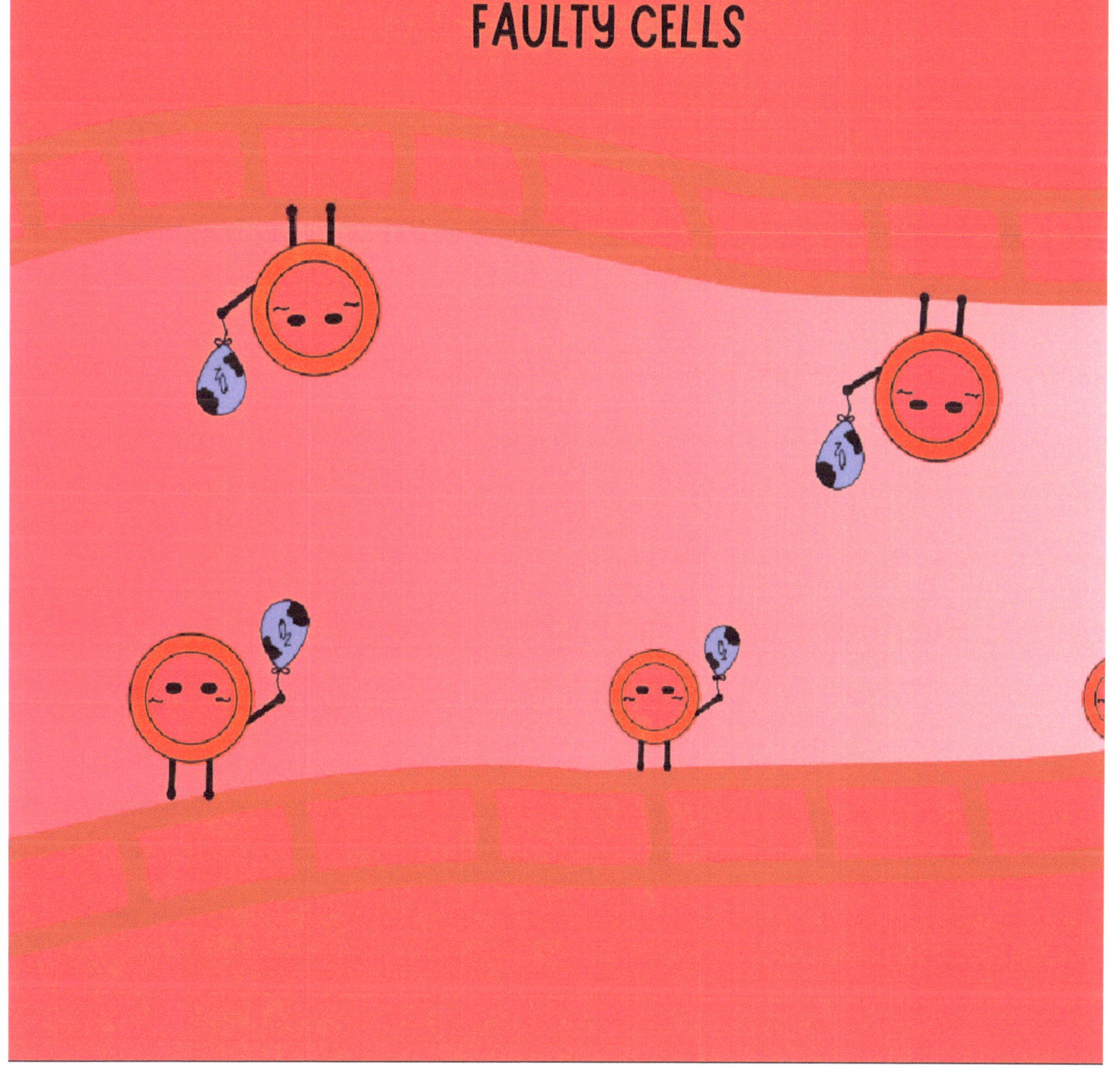

TOO FEW HEALTHY CELLS

Which causes cancer cells take over the bone marrow, so it can't produce enough cells

TOO MANY FAULTY CELLS

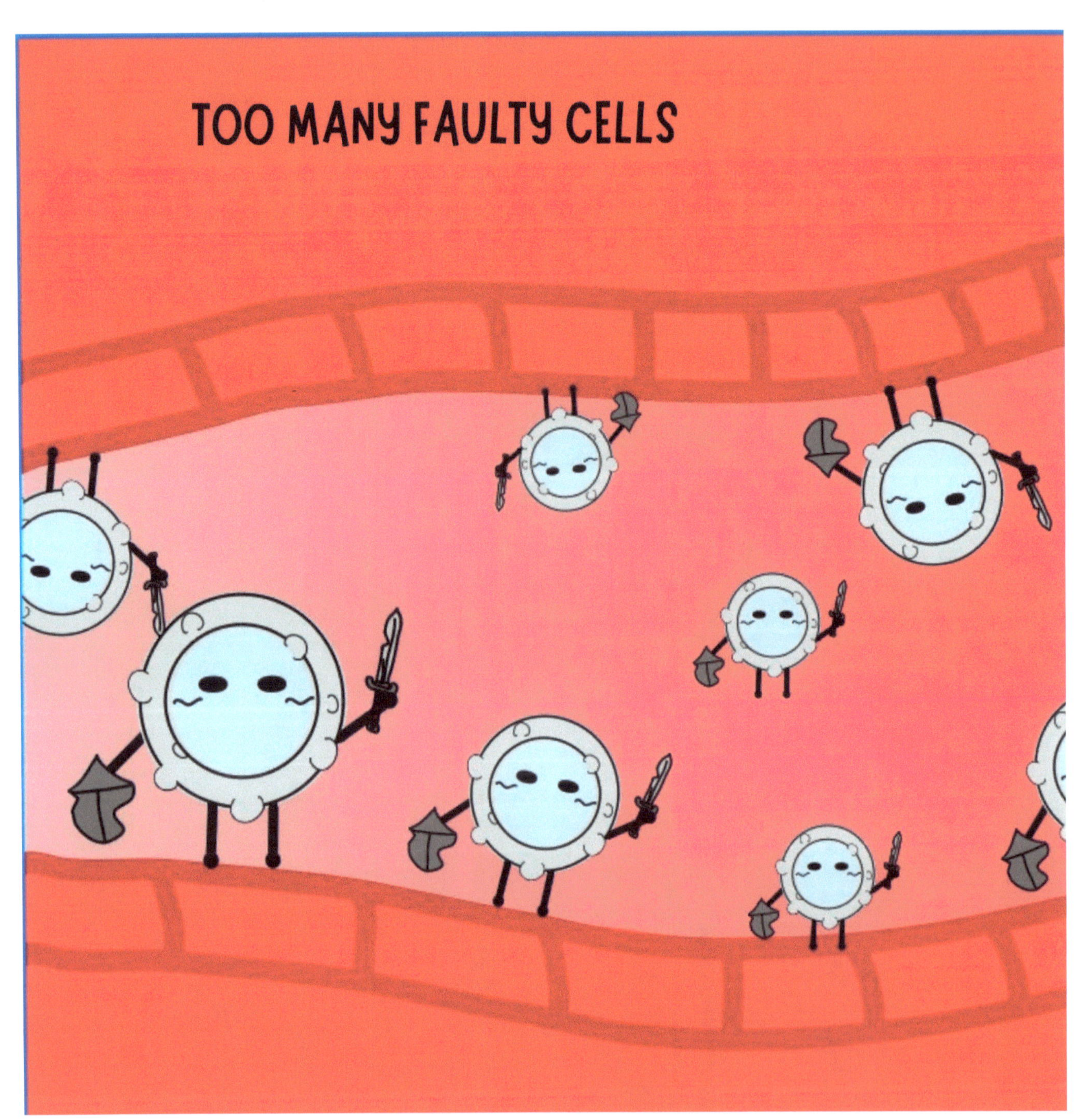

These cells don't work properly and crowd
out healthy cells

Blood cancer is treatable because of modern medicine
BYE!!

I've always believed that stories have the power to heal, just like medicine. I'm Shruti Maurya, a student and aspiring doctor, and I wrote this book to help spread awareness about cancer in a way that's engaging and easy to understand. Through my experiences volunteering at blood donation camps, interning in hospitals, and advocating for health education, I've seen how important it is to talk about these issues. I hope this book sparks enthusiasm in little children and brings a smile.